# EAT SMART

## A Guide To Good Health For Kids

# EAT SMART
## A Guide To Good Health For Kids

Written and Illustrated by
**DALE FIGTREE, Ph.D.**

**NEW WIN PUBLISHING, INC.**

5/99

Library of Congress Cataloging-in-Publication Data

Figtree, Dale.
   Eat smart : a guide to good health for kids / written and
illustrated by Dale Figtree ; with a foreword by John McDougall.
      p.   cm.
   Includes bibliographical references (p.   ).
   Summary: Explains how proper nutrition can build a healthy body
and discusses other health concerns such as sleep, hygiene, and exercise.
   ISBN 0-8329-0465-1 (hardcover) : $10.95
   1. Teenagers—Nutrition—Juvenile literature.  2. Children—
Nutrition—Juvenile literature.  3. Health—Juvenile literature.
[1. Nutrition.  2. Health.]   I. Title.
   RJ235.F54   1992
613'.0433—dc20                                     92-4550
                                                      CIP
                                                      AC

# DEDICATION

*For James, who provided the inspiration.*

# Table of Contents

# FOREWORD

Obesity is now an epidemic in children and adolescents and is on the rise. Estimates range from 10 to 30 percent of children are overweight, and as they grow older they grow fatter. Over the last 20 years likelihood of being overweight has almost doubled in some age categories. As a single intervention, efforts to reduce fat, including vegetable oil, intake will be the most effective step to prevent the onset of obesity in children and to permanently reverse the problem for the overweight child.

Exercise is also important. However, a high-fat, low-carbohydrate diet is the root of the problem, causing children to become so lethargic and sickly they lack the interest in and energy to exercise. Once this form of modern-day malnutrition is remedied with a diet based on carbohydrates (starches, vegetables and fruits), a progressive cycle of increased physical activity and effortless weight loss begins.

Complications associated with childhood obesity include high blood pressure, diabetes, elevated cholesterol and triglycerides, sleep disorders, hormone disorders, and skeletal diseases. The same rich foods that make them fat — the meats, dairy products, and vegetable oils — also cause acne, oily skin, arthritis, skin rashes, tonsil enlargement, sinusitis, ear infections, asthma, stomach pains, constipation, colitis, appendicitis, hemorrhoids, and bed wetting for many children. The early years of malnutrition from too much rich food lays the foundation for heart attacks, strokes, and cancer in the adult years. Unfortunately, the threat of illness and prevention of an early death are not likely to gain the attention of young people. They're invincible.

Important implications for people of this age include such problems as difficulty finding clothes to fit, teasing and name calling from peers, and problems with getting dates. Nothing is more important to a teenager than looking great. The promise of weight loss, improved complexion, and increased athletic performance by a change in diet are the keys to their motivation. Unfortunately, because of the prevalence of incorrect information on health and nutrition, most children have no more chance of permanent success at weight loss and improved health than their parents.

There is a tendency for fat babies to become fat children and fat children to grow into fat adults. If a child's palate is conditioned to the taste of fat then likely the child will become fat and continue to choose the same foods throughout life. Also, obesity runs in families, but the cause is not passed on by faulty genetic material. The foundations for obesity are laid down by the education a child receives on which foods to like, how to cook, and how active to be in life. In addition, overweight children tend to have a negative attitude toward physical activity, often "inherited" from their parents. But they didn't start out life with these bad habits. As a child, I remember telling my mother "I can't chew this hunk of meat." As she watched me struggle she would say, "Johnny, you have to get your protein." She should have said, "Of course you can't. You have the wrong kind of teeth for meat eating. Give it to the cat."

Because overweight children and adolescents suffer from social discrimination, both from family and peers, they are often defensive about their obesity and have a difficult time listening to helpful messages. *Eat Smart* by Dale Figtree is the means to open a child's mind to the cause and solution to their weight and health problems. Parents spend great time, money, and effort to provide their children with business and educational opportunities, and a proper moral upbringing only to send them out in the world to be fat and sick. Children deserve a legacy of excellent health from their parents. *Eat Smart* is the best way to help children and to help parents help their children gain the health and appearance they deserve for a lifetime.

JOHN McDOUGALL, M.D.
March, 1992

# PREFACE

As a Nutritionist, I have encountered many people with long ingrained dietary habits detrimental to their health. I was reminded repeatedly of how genuinely difficult it was for them to re-program their way of eating and in the case of young children, particularly so. Yet this is the time when life-long habits are being formed and dietary patterns established.

Recognizing the need to reach children before their habits become too deeply set, and believing in their natural desire to want to learn how things work, the idea of this book began to form.

Although the story is based on an overweight child, it is not about dieting, but rather about understanding. It's about helping all children to understand the effects their food choices have on their health and well-being. It's about presenting them with new, healthier, and delicious options for their meals. And ultimately, it's about encouraging children to realize their power to influence not only their health, but the whole of their lives.

If you are ill or on medication, do not attempt this diet without the supervision of a physician experienced in the effects of dietary change.

# EAT SMART

*A Guide To Good Health For Kids*

As a kid I was free . . . free to skateboard, free to play baseball — — —

— — — free to eat pizza, sweets, soda pop and ice cream.

Then when I was eleven, something weird started to happen. Suddenly my favorite jeans wouldn't zip up, and my baseball T-shirt seemed too small.

What's wrong with these stupid jeans? MOM! Are you shrinking my clothes?

The problem wasn't really my clothes getting smaller, I was getting bigger. Not taller, just wider . . .

After a while, I succeeded in dealing with this situation.

I bought bigger clothes — and I don't mean a little bigger. I'm talking really big.

The great thing about BIG clothes was that I didn't have to notice my expanding size, except, of course, when I undressed in front of the mirror.

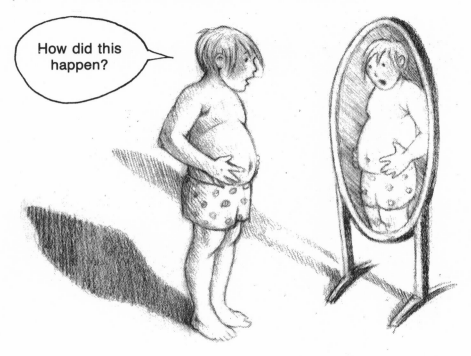

My body seemed to be changing before my eyes. My stomach developed rolls, my legs were beginning to look like tree trunks, and my neck kind of got lost in the fold of my chin.

The strange thing was the bigger I got, the hungrier I got.

Mom said, "Don't eat sweets!" Dad said, "Don't eat pizza!" Grandma said, "Not so many cakes!" This made me angry . . . so I ate even more!

By the time I was 13, the situation got really bad. Now my face was joining in the conspiracy against me . . . It started to break out!

Then came trouble at baseball practice. Before, I was always the first guy up to play. Slowly I was being pushed back to last. My batting hadn't really changed, it was just getting harder to make it around the bases . . . I seemed to be slowing down.

At school the nurse explained it when she weighed me. She said I was 15 pounds over-weight . . . which was like carrying around a big bag of potatoes wherever I went.

I couldn't stand it anymore. The day had come . . . I had to go on a DIET! I knew exactly what that meant . . . no cookies, no candy, no soda pop, no pizza.

The diet lasted about two days. I felt starved, deprived and depressed. I thought, maybe it's better to be fat than unhappy. So I went out and bought three chocolate bars, two bags of potato chips, a box of cookies and a double ice cream cone and ate the whole thing . . . immediately.

And that, and that, and that

Then I knew guilt.

Guilt I could live with, but not torture. Then came the day I was in the school swimming pool and Roxanne (the girl I had a crush on for two years) and her friend showed up. I couldn't get out of the pool, too embarrassed to be seen in a swim suit. After a long time in the water, I started getting really cold, and even shivering.

On top of that I was supposed to meet my Mom and I was already late. Then the worst happened. My Mom showed up . . . looking very, very mad. She demanded that I get out of the pool, instantly. I prayed to disappear, but since that didn't happen, I leaped out and grabbed a towel.

But the damage was done. The "beached whale" had been spotted.

The depression that followed caused my Mom to make some phone calls. Finally she told me we had an appointment to meet someone who could help me, someone called Johanna.

THANK GOD I MET JOHANNA!

Johanna was a nutritional counselor and a former fat person herself, though she sure didn't look it. She explained to me that DIETS DON'T WORK. They lead to feelings of being deprived and afterwards lead to eating even more than before.

Yes, I can relate to that.

She said that if you understand more about food and learn how to eat smart, you choose foods that not only taste good, but that are good for you. This includes treats, so that you don't feel deprived.

Then your body naturally adjusts itself to its best weight. That can mean losing, gaining or staying the same, depending on what your body needs.

I like the part about treats, but why do I need to know about food? Cave men didn't!

Johanna explained that cave men didn't need to understand about food because the food available then was good for their bodies.

But now things have changed. Many food companies create foods that are not good for the body which is why they are called JUNK FOOD . . . they are made of junk.

They usually contain large amounts of sugar, salt, artificial colors and flavors to trick people into liking them.

On top of that, huge amounts of money are spent putting ads on T.V., especially when kids are watching, to hypnotize people into wanting junk food even more.

The only way to protect yourself from this kind of trickery is to know more about what is in the food you eat. Then you can make better choices.

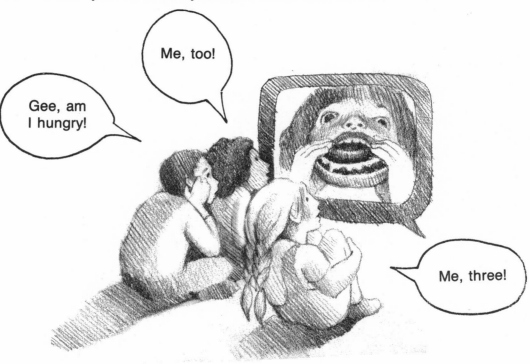

Well what actually is in the food I eat?

All food is made up of a combination of three food groups:

CARBOHYDRATES are the part of food that is used by the body primarily for energy. This energy actually comes from the sun. As the sun shines on plants, the plant cells trap the energy, like batteries. When we eat the plants our cells release the stored energy to be used to fuel and heat our bodies.

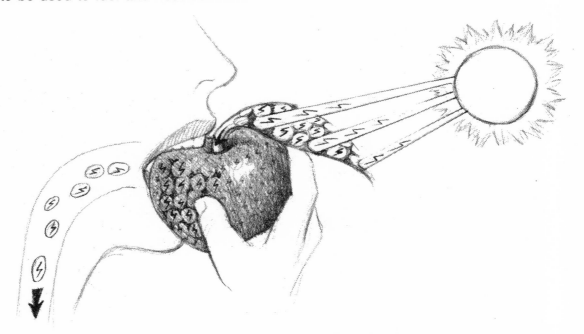

Another word for this energy is calories. A calorie is a way of measuring energy. All three food groups contain calories.

Carbohydrates are found in most foods, but the foods that contain the best quantities of carbohydrates are FRUITS, VEGETABLES, POTATOES, CORN, BEANS and WHOLE GRAINS (brown rice, whole wheat, oatmeal, etc.)

These are all called ENERGY FOODS. The fruit and vegetables provide quick even energy, the grains and beans provide long-lasting even energy.

You can consume substantial amounts of most carbohydrates without over eating of gaining extra weight. But when carbohydrates have been heavily processed, as with sugar and white flour, they become concentrated, higher-calorie foods that are easy to over eat.

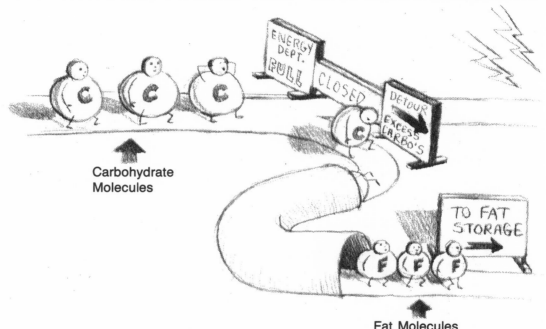

Carbohydrate
Molecules

Fat Molecules
(Triglycerides)

When you overeat and take in more of these calories than your cells can use, most of the excess is changed into fat and stored in fat deposits around the body.

FAT is another important nutrient but only required in small quantities. It is our secondary energy source, used after all carbohydrates have been burned.

Fat also has many other uses, such as padding and protecting the body, and making our skin waterproof.

If more fat is eaten than is needed by the body, the rest will be stored, causing fat deposits to become larger.

There is almost no end to the amount of fat the body can store.

Practically all food contains some fat. There are two different types:

SATURATED FAT — This is fat from animal products (meats, dairy, eggs, fish and chicken), which contain cholesterol. There is also saturated fat in coconut oil and palm oil, although they do not contain cholesterol.

Saturated fat and cholesterol intake can cause clogged arteries which lead to heart disease and strokes. This is responsible for half of all deaths in the U.S. each year.

UNSATURATED FAT — This is fat from most vegetables, nuts, seeds and avocados. This type of fat is healthier for the body and does not contain any cholesterol.

PROTEIN is the nutrient primarily used for building and repairing the body's tissues — organs, muscles, nerves, hair, and nails. Proteins also have many other important uses in our body, such as making up the antibodies used by our immune system to protect us from dangerous germs, and helping mend cuts with protein fibers.

The calories in protein can also be used for fuel, but only in severe emergencies, when there isn't enough carbohydrates or fat to burn. Protein is then taken from the muscles and changed into carbohydrates to be burned for energy. It's pretty amazing what the body can do.

Even though certain foods are called PROTEIN FOODS, there actually is protein in practically all food.

Meat and dairy products are high in protein but also high in saturated fat and calories.

Nuts and seeds are also high in protein, but they are high in unsaturated fat and calories.

Beans, legumes and certain grains are high in protein but low in fat. This makes them an excellent protein source.

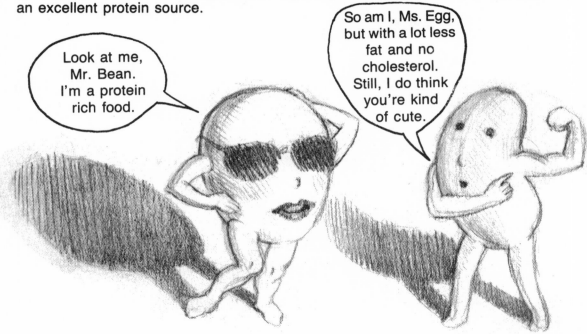

Look at me, Mr. Bean. I'm a protein rich food.

So am I, Ms. Egg, but with a lot less fat and no cholesterol. Still, I do think you're kind of cute.

Since most foods that are high in protein are also high in fat, what do you think happens if you eat large quantities of these foods?

Oh no!

**Right, extra weight!**

Diets very high in protein are also linked to other health problems including kidney and bone disease.

Besides carbohydrates, fats and proteins, food also contains VITAMINS, wonderful helpers in the body. They are substances which help cells to carry out specific tasks.

For example, Vitamin B$_{12}$ is needed for red blood cells to be able to divide and multiply. Vitamin K is needed for blood to clot. Vitamin A actually becomes part of the eye, making it possible for us to see. Vitamin C strengthens our immune system.

There are about 17 vitamins known at the present time and more being discovered every few years. Without them our bodies could not function.

At your service!

MINERALS are another necessary nutrient contained in most foods. They basically come from rocks and soil and are absorbed by plants. The plants then change them into a form that is easily digested by animals (including man) who eat the plants.

Each mineral helps the body in it's own way. Iron, for example, is a mineral that goes into red blood cells and acts as a magnet to attract oxygen molecules from the lungs. Certain minerals become electrically charged in the body and help conduct messages along nerves to the brain. Even the heartbeat is regulated by minerals.

If it weren't for the minerals calcium and phosphorus that make our bones strong, we would all look like jelly fish.

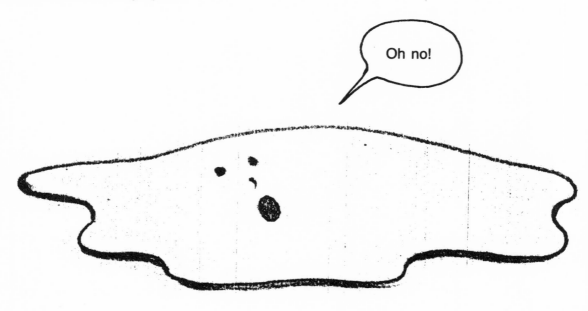

This may be a surprise, but WATER is actually the most important nutrient of all. We could live without food for three or four months, but without water, we would die in three or four days. Our body is made up of around 70% water, the same percentage as the earth.

Water is used in almost every cellular function. Water helps move food through the digestive system, it makes the blood liquid to carry nutrients to cells, it keeps us warm by insulating our flesh (water holds heat) and also cools us by carrying heat outside of our body through perspiration. Water cleanses our cells and carries waste out of the body.

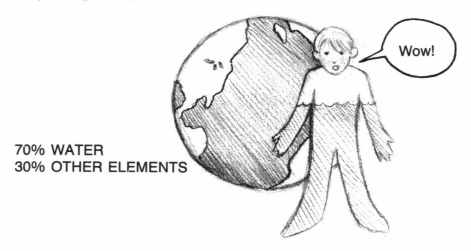

70% WATER
30% OTHER ELEMENTS

Besides drinking water, it is also important to eat foods that contain good quantities of water, basically fruits and vegetables. Most processed foods have the water cooked out of them.

FIBER is another important ingredient in food. It is the package that holds all the other nutrients together, and is left after all the other ingredients have been removed and digested.

Fiber is actually a carbohydrate, but one that we cannot digest and use for energy. Only termites can digest it because they produce a special digestive enzyme to break fiber down.

My favorite treat!

In the perfect plan of nature, termites break down dead tree fiber, enabling the tree's nutrients to go back to the soil.

If *we* can't digest fiber, why do we need it?

Fiber is important because it helps move the food through the digestive tract, exercising the intestines as it goes, so that they don't get lazy and weak. Along the way, fiber also picks up toxins, excess waste, water and fat and moves them out of the body.

If people eat food that is mostly lacking in good fiber, they may develop sluggish intestines and constipation, which can lead to digestive problems and disease.

Fiber is found in vegetables, fruit, nuts, grains and beans. Many processed foods have had the fiber removed from them, like white bread. Also, there is no fiber in meat, fish or dairy products.

Foods that contain the highest quantities of all of these necessary nutrients are natural foods. That means they are close to their original state, the way they were picked.

Once they are canned, bleached, or changed, the quantities of many nutrients are lessened or lost.

Heavily processed foods like sugar, white flour products (white breads, pastries, cookies and pasta), and many breakfast cereals, frozen foods, ice cream, candy and soft drinks, contain large amounts of empty calories.

Empty calories mean most of the vitamins and minerals have been lost in processing. Empty calorie food can actually rob the body's own vitamins and minerals, leaching them from tissues, bones and teeth.

Did you know a can of soda contains about seven teaspoons of sugar? That's a lot of empty calories!

Also, when you remove nutrients and change foods, they don't taste as good or look as good as they did before. That is why most food manufacturers then add chemicals to re-color, to add flavor, and also to preserve food so it can be on the supermarket shelf for a long, long time. Some foods are practically all chemicals, like colas and many brands of ice cream. They are actually fake food.

The body constantly measures the amount of nutrients you put in and if there are not enough, especially vitamins and minerals, it keeps craving more and more food. That's one of the reasons why many fat people are constantly hungry. They have more than enough calories, but not enough vitamins or minerals, so their body keeps telling them to eat more and more. If they only choose processed foods, the hunger never really goes away.

Most added chemicals are not one of the seven basic nutrients and cannot be used by the body in any helpful way. Some of those chemicals actually can hurt and poison cells. If the body cannot use these substances, it will try to get rid of them or store them. If the chemicals are harmful in any way, that could create disease later in life.

Ever since excess fat, sugar and chemicals have been added to foods, more people are getting cancer, asthma, heart disease and allergies. More teenagers are overweight and have aggravated skin problems.

To have a healthy looking and healthy working body, it is important to give it good quantities of the materials that it needs.

Would you put perfume in your Mom's car instead of gasoline?

Of course not! A car runs better on gasoline.

Why then would you put soda pop in your body if your body runs better on fresh juice?

This all made a lot of sense. I was willing to stay away from foods that were not good for my body, but the food I would have instead had to also taste good.

Johanna gave me a food program for breakfast, lunch and dinner. Some of the food I liked, and some of the food I never tasted before. But to loose weight, I was willing to try new things.

This included doing more exercise which Johanna said was also an important part of being healthy and fit.

Doesn't this form of arm exercise count?

Not only does exercise burn more calories, but it also helps clean the heart and arteries of fat deposits that can begin in childhood — plus it builds good strong muscles and actually can increase energy levels.

After two weeks on my new food program, I was amazed that I could really do it. I still thought about chocolate bars and ice cream, but I substituted that with healthier treats. I didn't really look very different, and that was frustrating, although my jeans were a little looser at the waist.

These orange juice ice pops your Mom made are rad.

After a month I was still on my program. A lot of the time it was easy, but there were times that were very hard. But I stuck to it and even increased my exercise more. I seemed to have extra energy and my weight continued to drop. Still, I didn't think I looked very different.

After three months I was amazed. I was no longer a fat kid. I was actually normal-sized. I'd check myself out in the mirror and watch the rolls disappear. On top of that, my skin was clearing up too!

Unbelievable.

I felt so strong that I could change myself that I started doing other things with more confidence.

At first I thought that I'd try the program for only a short time. Now I realize that eating smart and getting good exercise makes sense for most of the time.

Before, I thought I was free. But now, looking back, I realize I was trapped in my habits. I was trapped by T.V. commercials, by what other kids were eating and doing, by food I'd see in stores — I couldn't help myself. I had no choice but to junk out!

Now I have a choice. I pay attention to what I eat, and I still really enjoy food. When you feel good about yourself, in a way, that's really when you are free . . . free to get on with other things in life.

# QUESTIONS & ANSWERS FROM KIDS & PARENTS

**Are nuts and avocados too fattening to eat if I want to lose weight?**

If you are doing a "weight loss" diet of only low calorie foods, then nuts and avocados should be avoided. But, as I said earlier in the book, diets usually don't work. People feel hungry, deprived and resentful, then usually end up bingeing. It makes more sense to instead, eat balanced healthful meals that contain a mixture of low-calorie and high-calorie foods. You may lose weight a little slower, but you will be developing a new way of eating that will transform your body to it's healthiest state. In the long run it is best to develop new eating habits than to go on periodic diets.

Of course if losing weight is your concern, do not snack or over eat nuts, avocados, desserts, or any other high calorie food. They should only be a small part of a balanced meal.

**Will I ever be able to eat a chocolate bar or pizza again?**

Of course, but it should be something only to have on special occasions. When you begin a healthier way of eating, it's important to stay away from "junk foods" for a while to help the body break old habits and learn new ones. After that, having a small nibble once in a while should not disturb your progress. But be aware, sometimes a little taste can reawaken the addiction and it can take a lot of effort to free yourself again.

**If I remove milk or cheese from my diet, will I get enough calcium for my bones and teeth?**

Absolutely, if you eat nuts and lots of green vegetables you get all the calcium you need. Dairy products contain cholesterol and can produce excess mucus in the respiratory tract and sinuses, therefore, they are not the best source for getting calcium. Actually, calcium deficiency problems are caused more by things that drain calcium from the body, than from the amount eaten. Some of the things that drain calcium are soft drinks, coffee, aspirin and other drugs, and especially, too much protein in the diet.

**Without meat or dairy, will I get enough protein for a growing kid?**

New scientific evidence has shown that all people actually need a lot less protein than was originally estimated 20 years ago and that all the essential proteins we need are in most foods. Of course, some foods have more quantities of protein than others. If your diet contains good quantities of beans, grains, nuts and vegetables, you will get all the protein your body needs.

REMEMBER: Protein from animal sources comes with cholesterol and has no fiber. Also, laboratory experiments suggest that eating meat from animals that are given hormones to fatten them up, plus other drugs, may cause cancer in humans. On top of that, most animals today are raised in miserable conditions. Eating meat supports that cruel treatment.

## If I over eat healthy treats, can I get fat?

If you overdo anything, you will create a problem . . . so, the answer is yes. Treats should be considered occasional food because they can be higher in calories than other food. If you take in more calories than your body can burn, they will go into fat storage.

## Do I need protein when I am sick with a cold or fever?

It is impossible to not absorb some protein because it is in all food. But if you are ill, it is better to eat simple, easy-to-digest foods like fresh vegetable/fruit juices and blended vegetable soups. It is wise to stay away from the more complex foods until you are well. Resting is essential, and if you are resting, your calorie and protein needs are therefore much reduced. Also, during a cold it is important to eliminate all dairy and wheat products since they can produce excess mucus.

## Is all cholesterol bad for the body?

Some cholesterol is required by the body for hormone production. The liver produces all that we need without our having to eat foods that contain cholesterol.

## I find it almost impossible to stay away from junk food. What can I do?

Along with physical addiction, food cravings can also stem from mental and emotional addictions. I suggest working with both a nutritionist and a psychologist. The combination can provide both powerful support and insight into understanding yourself and the causes behind your actions. Joining groups like Overeaters Anonymous can also be helpful and very supportive.

### If I reduce my intake of animal products, do I risk a vitamin $B_{12}$ deficiency?

There is still much controversy about vitamin $B_{12}$. First of all, we actually only need very small quantities of this vitamin. Some scientists feel it is available only in animal products, others feel it is in some seeds and vegetables, while others believe we can produce traces of it in our lower intestine. Personally, I've never known a vegetarian with a $B_{12}$ deficiency. Cows and horses that eat only grass and grain don't have $B_{12}$ deficiencies. Where do they get it from? If you are worried, you could get a blood test from a lab to check your vitamin $B_{12}$ levels.


### What if I start to lose too much weight eating natural foods?

Some people, especially children, burn calories very quickly and therefore need a higher caloric intake. In that case I suggest increasing the quantities of foods you eat. You should increase nuts in the recipes by 1 or 2 oz., have more avocado with meals, snack on Trail Mix (dried fruit, raisins and raw nuts or seeds) when hungry and drink almond milk. Cold-pressed vegetable oils can also be used, but never more than 2 oz. per day.

Also, sometimes when people begin to eat a healthier diet, for the first month or two the body cleans out old stored toxins and breaks down old tissue. This usually causes weight loss. But after a few months the body increases building new tissue and then there is a slow gain to the body's best weight.

### Should I take vitamins with this program?

A diet high in vegetables, fruit, nuts and grain is packed with vitamins and minerals. Unless you have a problem with absorbing a particular nutrient, you can get all of your nutrients through a good variety of natural foods. Even with so-called depleted soils, plants won't grow unless the basic requirements of nutrients are available. Of course if organically grown food is available, that would be the best choice for highest nutrient and lowest pesticide levels.

### I need coffee to wake me up in the morning. Is this harmful?

The caffeine in coffee is a liver irritant. First thing in the morning, when the body is most sensitive, it is a harsh jolt, which many people think gives them more energy. Actually, the opposite is true. The body uses up it's own energy getting caffeine out of the system as fast as possible. That feels like a rush of energy, but in fact we have wasted energy dealing with it. Having a freshly made juice first thing in the morning gives the body a burst of carbohydrates which quickly get turned into a true energy that the body can run on.

### If I want to be an athlete, shouldn't I eat red meat?

You can get all of the necessary nutrients you need for strong muscles and high energy without eating meat. Of course you will need to eat large quantities of nuts and grains and beans and vegetables, but there are many athletes, Olympic Gold Medal winners among them, who are vegetarians. By the way, the strongest animals in the world are elephants, who eat only vegetable matter. That's true for gorillas, horses and cattle, too.

## Will an occasional egg for breakfast upset my food program?

If the bulk of your food intake is high fiber wholesome foods, occasional eggs should not create any problems. The eggs, though, should be from chickens raised in a healthy or organic way — without drugs and free-range. This means they are fed healthy chicken feed and are able to get exercise and sunshine. Most commercial chickens are instead, locked into small over-crowded cages in dark factories and fed a lot of hormones and drugs to fight diseases that breed in these unnatural and cruel conditions.

## Can I use olive oil on my salad?

All oils are high calorie, slow digesting food. But, if you are not overweight or have digestive difficulties, using a small amount of cold pressed* vegetable oil (olive, peanut, sesame, walnut, canola) should not be a problem as long as you do not use more than 2 oz. per day. Large amounts of fat intake, which includes unsaturated oils, has been linked to several kinds of cancer.

*The oil should be cold pressed because heat used in the pressing of oil destroys the natural vitamin E which keeps the oil fresh. Most commercial oils are processed with heat and require chemical preservatives added because there is no vitamin E left and it is too expensive to add back.

## Is margarine healthful to use?

Even though margarine is made from vegetable oil, it is put through a process of hydrogenation (passing hydrogen gas through the oil) which changes it's molecular structure. Some researchers believe this new structure may cause dangerous cell changes in the body after many years and that margarine should not be used.

**Can food affect my moods?**

Most definitely, yes! Many children become hyperactive and lose the ability to concentrate after eating sugar and chemical foods. Psychiatrists are now finding that many forms of mental illness improve with healthier dietary changes. Discover the effects for yourself. Pay attention to how you feel after eating different foods. Your own experience is the best way to learn.

**I've tried lower calorie natural food programs, but I don't seem to lose the weight I would like to. What can I do?**

When changing your diet from high-calorie processed foods to more low-calorie natural foods, the body can temporarily slow down using calories. It does this as a protective measure in case a famine is the cause of the lower calorie intake. This is why some people on diets do not lose very much weight. The way to give the body the message to speed up using calories is through good exercise.

*Eating a healthy diet means you consume less toxic chemicals. But beware, toxic chemicals can get into your body from sources other than food. Chemicals are in toothpaste, soaps, dish detergents, household cleaners and cleansers (especially for the bathroom and oven), hair spray, nail polish and nail polish remover, even laundry detergent. We are fortunate that now it is possible to buy all these products with less or no chemicals from health food stores and even some supermarkets. It is important to always read labels and find out what is in a product and choose the one least harmful to your body.

# EXERCISE TIPS

Exercise is one of the major ingredients in staying in good shape, physically, health wise and mentally. The more exercise, the stronger the muscles, the thicker the bones, the better the circulation, the clearer the mind.

A good exercise program is one that is consistent, at least three to five times per week. It's important to find a form of exercise that is enjoyable as well as being a good work-out. If not, the mind will eventually rebel and create resistance to wanting to do it. Exercising to music helps turn movement almost into a dance. Studying an Eastern form of exercise like karate, tai chi or yoga also helps to develop a kind of wisdom and awareness.

As important as exercise is, it is equally important to know when to rest. When feeling very tired and sluggish, which is different from lazy, or when going through a cold, or any illness, it is better to not exercise and instead rest or nap. The reason is simple. There is not enough energy available in the body for exercise at that time. It is being used someplace else in the body to do other work. Trust the body's wisdom. Listen to the body's message. If you go out and force exercise, you may feel temporarily better, but you may have robbed energy from some other place and interrupted important repair work.

# SKIN CARE

Teenage skin problems have several causes, from overproduction of oil glands, cleaning of the liver, higher levels of hormones to emotional stress. The results of these actions, namely blemishes, can be minimized and in many cases, eliminated, by making a few changes.

Keeping the surface of the skin clean of oil and bacteria buildup is the first step, by washing the face morning and night with a mild soap and a good washcloth or natural sponge. The texture of the cloth cleans deep down into the pores. For back break-outs, using a good back brush during each bath can help to clear it up.

Diet has a strong effect on the condition of the skin. Fried foods, fatty foods, chocolate and dairy products can aggravate skin problems and create excess skin oil. This is also true of heavily processed foods that are low in fiber. They lead to sluggish bowels which slow down removal of toxins from the body, creating a more toxic system, which in turn can contribute to developing blemishes.

On the other hand, foods with high water and high fiber contents, like fruit and vegetables, flush the system, keeping the digestion working quickly and efficiently, keeping the whole body clean. Vitamin A, which is high in carrots and other yellow and orange vegetables, and zinc, which is high in pumpkin seeds and grain, have been found to have beneficial healing effects on skin problems.

The emotional causes of skin problems are best dealt with by communication — expressing how we feel — letting others know what we need — trying to understand how the people around us feel. Sometimes it is a good idea to talk with a school guidance counselor who is there to help. Also, exercise may create a calming effect on strong emotions. If emotions are causing us continuous pain they need to be paid attention to the same way we would pay attention to a pain in our stomach or any other place, by seeking professional help.

*When it comes to caring for the skin, it is important to be aware of what you put on it. Skin medicines, make-up, creams and lotions many times contain chemicals that are not good for the body. When you put them on the skin, they seep into the system. If you wouldn't want to eat it, then don't put it on your skin. Buy only products with pure and simple ingredients that won't in any way irritate or pollute the body.

# THE EAT SMART PROGRAM

The most important thing about a good food program is to enjoy the taste of your food and to feel satisfied after meals, not feel hungry or deprived.

The following menus are full of delicious, easy-to-make, high-energy, high-nutrient meals. Remember, it's important to try new things or you'll never know what you are missing!

It's also important to eat good-size portions of food at each meal. Most of the food on this program is low and medium calorie, so that the few high calorie foods included are balanced. But be sure not to eat more of the higher calorie foods (nuts, avocados, desserts) than the program suggests if you need to lose weight.

Recipes for all the foods listed are in the next chapter.

# BREAKFAST

Begin with a glass (8 oz.) of Freshly Made Juice

Delicious juice combinations are apple-carrot-celery, orange-carrot, apple-cucumber, grape-celery, or any other fruit and vegetable combination that tastes good.

Using both fruit and vegetables in juice adds extra minerals and balances the sweetness.

A freshly made juice is your morning vitamin pill. Since it's digested very quickly, it produces almost instant energy and it's packed with nutrients . . . a great way to start a day!

Juice is followed by:

Fresh fruit salad (3 pieces)
topped with 1 oz. of ground or chopped nuts

The nuts should be raw and unsalted. Choose a different variety each day of either almonds, cashews, hazelnuts, pecans, sunflower seeds, or walnuts.

or:

A big bowl of whole grain cereal
with 2 pieces of chopped fruit

For creamy cereal cook with extra water or use ½ cup of fresh juice, rice milk or oatmeal banana milk.

For variety try oatmeal, corn meal, granola, millet, rice flakes or any other natural whole grain cereal made without sugar, flavorings, colorants or preservative chemicals.

Once a week you can have:

> 3 Apple-Corn Cakes with 100% Pure Fruit Preserves.

If you are in a rush, or not feeling very hungry try:

> A big glass of Breakfast Smoothie

These breakfasts are not only delicious, but they are packed with an excellent combination of nutrients and produce a strong even energy that lasts several hours.

If you are hungry at mid-morning have a banana or other fruit.

# LUNCH

Sandwich with Small Salad or Salad Sticks, Fruit

or

Large Salad with nuts, 2 Pieces of Fruit

or

Soup and Salad.

Choices include:

Mexican Bean Burrito or Tostada
Oriental Burrito (Mu Shu Vegetable Roll)
Juicy Vegie Burger
Salad Pita Pocket with Bean Spread
Almond Butter and Sliced Banana Sandwich
Guacamole Pita Pocket/or Sandwich
Garden Salad with Sunflower Seeds
Crunchy Apple, Carrot and Walnut Salad
Spinach Salad with Mandarin Oranges and Pecans
Hearty Soup with whole grain roll, Salad

For lunch dessert have one or two pieces of your favorite fruit.

\* \* \* \* \*

If you are hungry after school, try one of these snacks: air popped pop corn, fruit juice ice pop, banana or strawberry ice cream, a smoothie, or rice cakes with 100% pure fruit preserves.

# DINNER

A glass of (8 oz.) Fresh Vegetable Juice*

*tomato/celery/lemon (tastes like V8)
carrot/celery/slice of beet (mildly sweet, pretty color)
cucumber/celery/mint (very cool)

followed by:

Big Mixed Salad with 2 tbsp. of home-made Dressing

followed by:

Main Courses

Juicy Vegie Burgers with oven-baked "French Fries"
Vegetable Lasagna
Lee Ho Chungs Oriental Rice and Vegies
One-Pot Rice and Vegies
Potato Croquettes
Spaghetti Marinara (with whole grain or corn pasta)
Spaghetti Squash Pasta with Ratatouille
Mexican Bean and Rice Burritos or Tostadas
Orange Mashed Yams, Steamed Vegetables with Lemon Sauce
Baked or Mashed Potatoes and Steamed Vegetables with Rich Brown Onion
    Gravy
Shepherd's Pie
Quick Chili
Hearty Soups

About dessert — sweet foods generally do not mix well with complex dinner foods. If you are hungry one or two hours after you eat, then have one portion of a treat.

## TREATS

It takes a while for old cravings to disappear, but it helps if other, more healthy "treats" can take the place. There are many delicious treats that are also good for you.

Popcorn, air popped with low salt vegetable seasoning
Fruit Juice Ice Pops
Banana or Strawberry Ice Cream with Blackberry Sauce
Rice Cakes with 100% Pure Fruit Preserves
Banana Pudding
Homemade Tortilla Chips and Salsa

## SPECIAL OCCASION TREATS

Banana Nut Bar
Apple Nut Cake
Apple Pie

# DRINKS

Smoothies
Natural Soda Pop
Sweetened Rice Milk
Oatmeal Banana Milk
Almond Milk

# RECIPES

You can still have many of the foods you love, you just have to learn to prepare them in a more healthful way. That is what many of these recipes are about.

If there are any ingredients you strongly dislike, leave them out or substitute something else. Be creative.

## BREAKFAST SMOOTHIE
1 serving

1 cup (8 oz.) fresh fruit and vegie juice
1 banana or persimmon (if in season)
12 almonds, cashews, hazelnuts, or 2 oz. of sunflower seeds

Make juice first. Then blend nuts dry in blender. Add juice and banana and blend again about one or two minutes until smooth. Drink slowly!

# CREAMY CINNAMON BANANA OATMEAL

### 1 serving

2½ cups water
1 cup oatmeal
½ tsp. cinnamon
¼ tsp. nutmeg
1 banana
1 tbsp. raisins, optional

Bring water to boil. Add all the ingredients. Cover and simmer for five minutes. Let sit covered for two minutes.


# CORN-APPLE CAKES

1 cup corn meal
½ cup garbanzo flour
1 cup grated apple
1 cup apple juice
1 tsp. honey
1 tbsp. apple sauce
1 tsp. cinnamon

Combine dry ingredients. Combine wet ingredients. Mix together, stirring well. Cook on a non-stick griddle and turn when bubbles form on top and edges begin to dry. Serve with 100% fresh fruit preserves.

Courtesy of The McDougall Health-Supporting Cookbook, Volume I

# RICE MILK

1 cup cooked brown rice  
2 cups water  

1 tsp. vanilla  
1 tsp. maple syrup or honey  

Blend until very smooth. Put in quart size bottle. Add another 2½ cups of water. Shake well. This keeps in the refrigerator for several days.

# OATMEAL BANANA MILK

4 cups water  
2 cups cooked oatmeal  

1 ripe banana  
1 tsp. vanilla  

Combine all ingredients and blend until smooth. Refrigerate and shake before using.

Courtesy of The McDougall Health-Supporting Cookbook, Volume I

# ALMOND MILK

2 oz. raw almonds  
1 cup of water  

a few drops of vanilla  
½ tsp. maple syrup  

Place almonds in blender and grind to a powder. Add water and blend for a few minutes. Strain through a fine strainer.

# SANDWICH SPREADS

For sandwiches use whole grain bread, whole wheat pita pockets or whole wheat or corn tortillas.

Add lettuce, tomato and sprouts to sandwiches for an extra burst of crunch and nutrients.

## BEAN BURRITO or TOSTADA

**Bean Spread**
1 cup cooked beans (kidney, pinto, or red)
1 clove garlic
1 tsp. ground cumin
3 tbsp. water
1 tsp. low sodium tamari

Place all ingredients in a food processor or blender and process until smooth. Add more water if mixture is too thick.

For one Burrito:

whole wheat tortilla or chapati, steamed
½ cup of Mexican Bean Dip
¼ cup Salsa (look under Sauces)
1 lettuce leaf, shredded
sprouts

Spread Mexican Bean Dip on whole wheat tortilla. Add Salsa or finely chopped tomatoes, shredded chopped lettuce and sprouts. Wrap chapati on both sides and roll closed on one end.

For a tostada, spread beans on steamed corn tortilla. Cover with remaining ingredients, topping it with salsa.

Two burritos or tostadas make up one meal.

## MU SHU VEGETABLE (ORIENTAL VEGIE ROLL)

Serves 1

2 whole wheat chapatis or tortillas, steamed
½ cup bean sprouts
½ cup broccoli, chopped
½ cup mushrooms, chopped
2 leaves of bok choy, chopped
½ cup green pepper, chopped
2 stalks of celery, chopped
1 cup brown rice
ginger tamari sauce

Steam all vegetables together for 10 minutes until soft. Place a scoop of brown rice ona tortilla, then put half the cooked vegetables on top of that. Top with 2 tbsp. ginger tamari sauce. Fold two sides of chapati together and roll other end closed. Repeat same for second tortilla.

# GINGER TAMARI SAUCE

¾ cup hot water
1 tbsp. honey
2 tbsp. low sodium tamari or soy sauce
1 tsp. ginger (grated fresh or powdered)
1 tsp. paprika
⅛ cup rice vinegar

Blend water, honey, tamari, ginger and paprika. Then add vinegar and blend again. Refrigerate leftover sauce to be used on rice or other dish.

# JUICY VEGIE BURGER

Serves 2

1 cup lentils
3 cups water
1 onion, finely chopped
1 clove garlic, crushed

1 carrot, grated
½ cup bulgur wheat
2 tbsp. ketchup or tomato sauce
1 tsp. mustard

Bring lentils and water to a boil. Add onions, garlic and carrot. Reduce heat, cover and simmer for 30 minutes. Add remaining ingredients. Cook an additional 15 minutes. Shape into patties and put under broiler until browned on top. Turn and brown bottom and serve with lettuce and tomato and ketchup (without sugar). Can also be served in a whole wheat pita pocket or whole wheat roll.

Courtesy of The McDougall Health-Supporting Cookbook, Volume I

# SALAD PITA with BEAN SPREAD
## Serves 1

2 leaves lettuce, shredded
1 tomato, chopped
½ small red pepper, chopped
1 carrot, grated
½ onion, finely chopped

Mix together all ingredients. With 1 cup of prepared bean spread, scoop half into pita pocket. Fill with half of mixed ingredients. Top with sprouts. Repeat with second pita pocket.

For a juicier sandwich pour 1 tbsp creaming dressing (under salad dressings) into filled pita.

The following two sandwiches are a little higher calorie and should not be eaten more than once a week.

# ALMOND BUTTER AND SLICED BANANA
## Serves 1

Spread ⅓ cup nut butter on whole grain bread. Add banana slices or 100% fruit jam. Other nut butters can be substituted such as cashew, sunflower, hazelnut or peanut butter. Be sure there are no other added ingredients in nut butter or fruit jam.

## GUACAMOLE (Avocado Spread) PITA POCKET

### Serves 2

1 ripe avocado, mashed
1 tbsp. lemon juice
1 clove garlic, crushed
1 small tomato

½ small onion, finely chopped
1 small carrot, grated
stone ground mustard
whole wheat pita pocket

Blend all ingredients together until smooth. Spread mustard on inside of pita pocket. Stuff with half of mixture, adding chopped lettuce and green sprouts on top.

## RAINBOW GARDEN SALAD with SUNFLOWER SEEDS

The Rainbow Garden Salad can have an assortment of the following ingredients. Experiment with different combinations.

Green lettuce or spinach (any type except iceberg lettuce, which has less nutrients)

ripe tomatoes
cucumber (peel if waxed)
red or green bell pepper
spring onions
grated carrot
grated red or white cabbage
sprouts

mushrooms
corn
onion
grated raw or cooked beets
avocado (occasionally instead of nuts)
and any other raw vegetable you like

For variety try chopping the ingredients into very small pieces or putting them into a blender and making a gazpacho. Try making salads of different color combinations — like a red and orange salad made with red pepper, carrots, red cabbage, beets, radishes and an orange. Besides tasting good, it's lovely to look at!

Added to the salad to balance the nutrients should be 2 or 3 ounces of nuts or seeds. Sunflower Seeds and Pumpkin Seeds both taste great in salads. Pumpkin Seeds are high in Zinc which is especially good for the skin. Even though nuts are high in unsaturated fat calories, by combining them with a salad you still have a normal calorie meal . . . One that is also high in fiber, vitamins, minerals with a healthy portion of protein, too.

## CRUNCHY APPLE, CARROT, WALNUT SALAD
1 serving

1 yellow apple, peeled and chopped, covered with lemon juice
1 carrot, grated
1 stalk of celery, chopped
¼ cup raisins
2 oz. raw walnuts, chopped
2 leaves of lettuce, finely shredded

Mix all above ingredients together and serve with 2 tbsp. Honey, Nut Butter Dressing. (Look under salad dressings)

# SPINACH SALAD WITH MANDARIN ORANGES AND PECANS
## Serves 2

10 leaves of spinach, washed and torn into smaller pieces
½ small red onion, sliced
4 mushrooms, sliced
2 Mandarin oranges or tangerines, sectioned
½ cup raw pecans or walnuts, coarsely chopped

Mix all ingredients together and serve with Honey Nut Butter Dressing.


# SALAD DRESSINGS and SAUCES

Many Health Food Stores now carry a good variety of delicious "non-oil" salad dressings (easier to digest and less calories than oil dressings). Remember to read ingredient labels, making sure the dressing is all natural, without added chemicals.


## TANGY DRESSING FOR SALADS
### Serves 2

1 tomato
juice of 1 lemon
½ small onion

½ cup water
1 clove of garlic, crushed
pinch of oregano, dill and thyme

Mix together in blender and serve. You can make a larger amount and store it in the refrigerator for two or three days.

## CREAMY DRESSING FOR SALADS

1 cup of cooked beans (garbanzo, white or red)
2 cloves garlic
juice of 1 lemon
½ tsp. cumin
½ cup water
1 tbsp. low sodium tamari

Mix all ingredients in blender until smooth. Add extra water if too thick. Should a be creamy but pourable consistency. Serve 2 tbsp. per serving. Store remaining dressing in refrigerator for two or three days.

## HONEY NUT BUTTER DRESSING

2 oz. of tahini or peanut butter
juice of ½ lemon
1 tsp. honey
water to thin to a creamy, pourable consistency

Blend ingredients together and pour over salad.

# SALSA

3 tomatoes, finely chopped or 1 can (14 oz) tomatoes
1 medium onion, finely chopped
⅛ cup finely chopped mild chiles
small bunch of fresh cilantro, chopped, or 1 tsp. dried cilantro
1 tsp. tamari or 1 oz. sea salt

Mix together all ingredients and serve as a dip or a dressing on salads or use in burritos or tostadas.

# BROWN ONION GRAVY

1 small onion, chopped
2¼ cups water
1 tsp. low-sodium tamari
1 tsp. miso (soy bean paste)
    or extra tsp. tamari

½ tsp. mustard powder
1 tsp. dried thyme
1 bay leaf
2 tbsp. cornstarch or arrowroot

Saute onions in saucepan with ¼ cup water over medium heat for five minutes. Add remaining water and spices. Mix cornstarch with small amount of cold water to make a smooth white liquid. Slowly add to sauce, stirring as you do so. Continue to stir until thickened.

Optional: ¼ lb mushrooms can also be added in the beginning, sauted with onion.

## LEMON SAUCE FOR VEGETABLES

juice of 1 lemon
1 clove garlic, crushed
pinch of mint leaves
¼ cup of water

Put all ingredients into a jar and shake well.


# HEARTY SOUPS

### TANGY LENTIL LEMON SOUP

1 cup lentils
3 cups water
1 onion, chopped
1 carrot, chopped
1 stalk celery, chopped
1 tbsp. tamari
Juice of lemon

Bring lentils and water to a boil and cook for 10 minutes. Then add other ingredients except lemon. Cover and simmer until lentils are soft. (About 45 mintues to 1 hour.) Add lemon juice to give it a tangy flavor and bring out the natural saltiness.

If lentils cause you gas, soak raw lentils in water overnight. Change water in morning and proceed with recipe.

# CREAMY VEGETABLE SOUP

1 carrot, chopped
1 onion, chopped
1 stalk of celery, chopped
1 zucchini, chopped
1 stalk broccoli, chopped
2 stalks chard, chopped

2 tomatoes, and any other
   vegetable you would like
1 tbsp. tamari or miso
small handful of fresh dill or parsley
water to cover all of the vegetables
Juice of 1 lemon

Put all ingredients, except lemon, into a large pot. Bring to boil then cover and simmer for 45 minutes. Put cooked soup in food processor or blender and blend until creamy. Add lemon juice. (Lemon juice is actually a salt substitute. It brings out the salty flavors in food.)

# ITALIAN MINESTRONE SOUP

1 onion, chopped
1 carrot, chopped
1 stalk of celery, chopped
3 tomatoes, chopped
1 cup of whole wheat macaroni

5 cups of water
1 clove garlic
1 bay leaf
2 tbsp. oregano

Saute onion and garlic in small amount of water. Add remaining ingredients, except macaroni. Bring to boil, cover, then simmer for 30 minutes. Add macaroni and simmer another 20 minutes and serve.

# CREAMY BUTTER BEAN SOUP

1½ cups dried butter beans, soaked overnight
6 cups of water
3 tomatoes (small, roma) chopped
1 small onion, chopped
1 large carrot, chopped
1 stalk of celery, chopped
1 tbsp. low sodium tamari or miso (soy bean paste)
bunch of parsley, finely chopped

Soak beans overnight. When ready to cook, rinse soaked beans. Put in a pot with 6 cups of water and boil for 10 minutes. Then cover and simmer for 45 minutes. Add remaining ingredients and continue to simmer, uncovered, until beans are tender and water is reduced (about 45 minutes).

# THICK AND DELICIOUS SPLIT PEA SOUP

1 cup split peas
4 cups water
1 onion, chopped
1 carrot, chopped
1 stalk of celery, chopped
1 tbsp. tamari
1 bay leaf

Bring split peas and water to a boil. Add other ingredients. Cover and simmer until split peas are soft (about 1½ hours).

# MAIN COURSES

## JUICY VEGETABLE BURGERS
## WITH OVEN-BAKED FRENCH FRIES

Vegetable burgers are listed under sandwiches.

### Oven-baked French Fries
Serves 4

4 large potatoes

Slice each potato lengthwise in ¼ inch slices. Place on oven rack in hot oven (450 degrees). Bake 15 to 20 minutes, until potato slice browns and expands. Serve hot with natural (sugar-free) ketchup.

## VEGETABLE LASAGNA CASSEROLE
Serves 4

4 potatoes
2 eggplant
2 cups tomato puree with oregano and garlic

2 zucchini
1 cup sliced mushrooms

Slice all vegetables lengthwise in ¼ inch slices. Oil a casserole dish and place slices of potatoes on the bottom. Then place slices of eggplant next. Spread over 1 cup of tomato puree. Place mushrooms on next. Finish with a layer of sliced zucchini. Spread remaining tomato puree over that. Sprinkle with ½ cup of water, cover and bake in 400 degree oven for 1 hour.

## LEE HO CHUNGS ORIENTAL VEGETABLES AND RICE

### Serves 4

2 cups brown rice
4 cups water
¼ cup bean sprouts
½ cup broccoli, chopped
¼ cup mushrooms, chopped

2 leaves of bok choy, chopped
½ green pepper, chopped
1 stalk of celery, chopped
½ cup ginger tamari sauce

Wash rice and place in pan with water. Bring to a boil, stir, cover and simmer. After 15 minutes add the remaining ingredients. Continue cooking until rice is finished (about about 15 minutes). Sprinkle with Ginger Tamari sauce.

Optional: Small scoup of Guacamole over vegetables

## ONE-POT RICE AND VEGIES

### Serves 4

2 cups brown rice
4 cups water
1 carrot, chopped
1 spring onion, chopped
4 mushrooms, chopped

1 stalk celery, chopped
½ cup peas, fresh or frozen
1 zucchini, chopped
1 bay leaf
pinch of oregano

Bring water to a boil. Add rice, cover and simmer 15 minutes. Add remaining ingredients and simmer until rice is cooked (about another 20 minutes). Remove bay leaf and serve.

# SPAGHETTI SQUASH PASTA with RATATOUILLE

## Serves 4

Spaghetti squash can be used instead of pasta. It's low calorie and high in nutrients and looks and tastes like pasta. Cut a big squash in half and steam until tender. When finished, gently pull out strands with a fork and serve topped with Ratatouille.

## Ratatouille

2 cups fresh tomatoes, chopped
    or 1 (16 oz.) can
1 large eggplant,
    chopped into ½ inch cubes
2 zucchini, chopped in ½ inch cubes
8 oz. mushrooms, chopped

1 carrot, chopped in small cubes
1 tsp. oregano
1 bay leaf
2 cloves garlic, crushed
½ cup water

Place all ingredients into a saucepan, bring to a boil, cover and simmer for 45 minutes.

# SPAGHETTI WITH MARINARA SAUCE

## Serves 4

1 pound of corn pasta or whole wheat pasta (spaghetti or macaroni)

Cook pasta in boiling water until just tender. Rinse in warm water. Add sauce and serve.

# MARINARA SAUCE

8 fresh tomatoes (roma)
   or 16 oz. can of plum tomatoes
1 small onion, chopped
2 cloves garlic, crushed
1 zucchini, chopped

½ cup mushrooms, sliced
1 tsp. oregano
1 tbsp. low sodium tamari
¼ cup water

Saute onions and garlic in water for five minutes. Add remaining ingredients. Cover and simmer for 30 minutes.

# POTATO CROQUETTES
### Serves 4

4 lg. potatoes, washed and cut into chunks
¼ cup water
½ cup peas, fresh or frozen
1 large carrot, chopped
½ onion, finely chopped
1 tsp. low sodium tamari
pinch of thyme

Steam potatoes until soft. Saute onions and carrots in water until almost soft (around 8 minutes). Add peas and thyme and cook another few minutes. Mash potatoes with water. Add remaining ingredients. Form into 2½ inch wide patties and place under broiler. Broil until slightly browned on top.

# BEAN AND RICE BURRITO

### Serves 2

4 whole wheat tortillas
  or chapatis, steamed
2 cups Mexican Bean Dip
2 cups cooked brown rice
1 cup salsa

4 leaves of lettuce, shredded
1 carrot grated
sprouts
Optional: ½ cup guacamole

Spread ½ cup of bean mixture and ½ cup rice on each tortilla. Cover with ¼ cup of salsa. Top with shredded lettuce, grated carrots and sprouts. Fold sides of tortilla together and roll over and serve. If guacamole is used, it should be placed between the rice and salsa.


# ORANGE MASHED YAMS
# AND STEAMED VEGETABLES WITH LEMON SAUCE

### Serves 4

4 medium sized yams
4 oranges
Optional: ½ cup chopped pineapple, 2 oz. chopped walnuts

Steam yams until tender. Peel skins. Cut oranges in half and scoop out pulp. In blender combine orange pulp and yams and blend until smooth. Mix in remaining ingredients and serve. For a fancier dish, scoop mixture back into orange halves, top with half a walnut and place under broiler for 10 minutes, until slightly browner.

## Steamed Vegetables with Lemon Sauce

Choose up to 3 pounds of two or more vegetables. Different colors insure a good variety of nutrients and an attractive color combination. It is best to steam vegetables as whole as possible because this preserves the most vitamins. After they are cooked they can be cut into smaller pieces. Most vegetables only take about 8 to 10 minutes to steam. Kale takes 20 minutes, but it's worth the wait. After cooked, pour lemon sauce over vegetables and serve.

## QUICK CHILI
### Serves 4

½ cup water
2 onions, chopped
1 green pepper, chopped
1 stalk celery, chopped
1 clove garlic, crushed

4 cups (32 oz.) fresh
    or canned tomatoes
4 cups cooked kidney beans
2 tbsp. chili powder
2 tsp. ground cumin

Place water, onions, green pepper, celery and garlic in a medium sauce pan and saute over high heat for 3-4 minutes. Add remaining ingredients, bring to a boil, reduce heat and cook gently for another 25 minutes or so to blend flavors. Stir occasionally. Serve over brown rice or baked potatoes.

Courtesy of The McDougall Health-Supporting Cookbook, Volume I

## MASHED POTATOES and STEAMED VEGIES
## WITH BROWN ONION GRAVY

### Serves 4

4 medium potatoes, peeled and cut into large chunks
1 medium onion, chopped
2 cloves garlic, crushed
2 tbsp. chopped parsley
½ tsp. basil
½ tsp. thyme

Place all ingredients into saucepan and add water to cover. Bring to a boil. Cover and cook over medium heat until done, about 30 minutes. Drain and reserve the cooking liquid. Add one cup hot cooking liquid back to the pot. Beat the cooked vegetables with electric mixer until smooth.

For steam vegies follow previous recipe. Serve both mashed potatoes and vegies with brown onion gravy. (Look under Dressings and Sauces)

Courtesy of The McDougall Health-Supporting Cookbook, Volume I

# SHEPHERD'S PIE
## Serves 4

4 medium potatoes,
    cooked in 2 inches of water until soft
paprika
1 onion, finely chopped
½ cup water
1 lb. broccoli, finely chopped
4 stalks of chard, chopped

1 bell pepper, finely chopped
3 medium carrots, finely diced
¾ cup chopped tomatoes
1 bay leaf
½ tsp. basil
1 tbsp. low sodium tamari

Saute onion in ½ cup water for 3 minutes. Add broccoli, pepper, carrots, basil, bay leaf and tomatoes. Mix well, cover and simmer 15 minutes. Then stir in chard and tamari. Put in 9″ × 13″ baking dish. Mash potatoes with small amount of cooking water and a dash of tamari and spread on top of vegetable mixture. Sprinkle with paprika and bake 15 minutes in 350 degree oven.

# TREATS

## POPCORN

Use an air popper if possible, then no oil is necessary for popping. You can also pop popcorn in a microwave oven, but be sure to get microwave popcorn that doesn't contain a lot of chemicals.

For seasoning use low-sodium vegetable powder, nutritional yeast powder, or granulated kelp powder.

## FRUIT ICE POPS

4 oranges, juiced

Use plastic ice pop molds or an ice cube tray and tooth picks. Pour in orange juice and freeze.

Try orange juice with mashed strawberries, or pineapple juice, watermelon juice, or any other fruit juice you can imagine. Oh Yes!

# BANANA OR STRAWBERRY ICE CREAM
## with BLACKBERRY SAUCE
### Serves 2

4 ripe bananas
½ cup water

Peel bananas and place in a plastic container and freeze. When ready to use, slice into 1 inch pieces and put in blender or food processor with water and blend until smooth. Serve immediately.

For strawberry ice cream use half banana, half frozen strawberries. Blend with water and serve.

For Blackberry Sauce: Thaw 1 cup of frozen blackberries, blend until smooth and pour over ice cream. Other delicious toppings are frozen strawberries, granola, chopped almond, and fresh fruit.


# BANANA CREAM PUDDING
### Serves 2

4 ripe bananas

Place in blender and blend until smooth. Serve immediately.

## TORTILLA CHIPS AND SALSA

Cut one or two whole wheat tortillas into small pie-shaped slices. Place on a cookie sheet and bake 10 minutes in a 350 degree oven. Remove and let cool and harden. For Salsa look under Dressings and Sauces.

# TREATS FOR SPECIAL OCCASIONS

## APPLE JACK BREAD

5 apples, peeled, quartered,
    and cored
1 cup raisins
1 cup water
1 tbsp. lemon juice
1 tbsp. ground cinnamon
1 tsp. ground nutmeg

½ tsp. ground cloves
1 cup oats, finely ground*
1 cup whole wheat flour
½ cup almonds, finely ground*
1 tsp. baking soda
1 tbsp. baking powder
    (without aluminum)

Pre-heat oven to 350 degrees. In saucepan combine apples, raisins, lemon, water and spices. Cook over medium heat until apples are tender and liquid is reduced by half. Set aside until cooled.

Combine remaining dry ingredients in separate mixing bowl. Combine dry mixture with cooled apple mixture. Pour batter into 8-inch, non-stick or oiled bread pan. Bake in oven for about 1 hour.

*Almonds and oats can be ground in blender or food processor with steel "S" blade.

Courtesy of Simply Good Cookbook

# CAROL'S APPLE PIE

2 cups of date pieces rolled in oat flour
1 cup chopped pecans
1 tsp. unsprayed orange rind, grated

For pie crust, cover above ingredients with juice from ½ an orange. Combine in food processor or blender with 1 cup of soft dates with pits removed. Add orange juice as needed. Oil a pie tin and press above mixture into it.

6-8 pippin or gala apples, peeled, cored and sliced thinly
juice of ½ orange
1 tsp. unsprayed orange rind, grated
½ cup date sugar
½ cup currants
½ tsp. cinnamon
½ tsp. coriander

For filling, mix all ingredients together and place in crust, sprinkle with date sugar and refrigerate until ready to serve. Serve within a few hours with banana ice cream.

# BANANA OATMEAL NUT BAR

1 cup ground rolled oats
2 ripe bananas
½ cup apple juice concentrate
¼ cup water
¼ cup chopped walnuts

Combine bananas and juice. Add enough rolled oats to make the consistency of oatmeal cookies. Press into no-stick or oiled rectangular baking dish. Bake at 350 degrees for 10 minutes.

Courtesy of Simply Good Cookbook

# DRINKS

## SMOOTHIES

1 banana
1 cup apple juice
½ cup frozen fruit (strawberries, blueberries, peaches, etc.)
    or chopped fresh fruit (papaya, mango, peach, pear, etc.)

Blend until smooth.

# NATURAL SODA POP

1 cup orange juice, cranberry juice, or other fruit juice
1 cup cold carbonated water or low sodium club soda
Ice cubes

Mix together and enjoy.

# SUGGESTED READING

For more great easy-to-make, delicious and nutritious recipes, I suggest the following cookbooks:

THE McDOUGALL HEALTH-SUPPORTING COOKBOOK, Volumes One and Two, by Mary McDougall, New Win Publishing, P.O. Box 5159, Clinton, NJ

SIMPLY GOOD, from The Center For Chiropractic and Conservative Therapy, Inc., 4310 Lichau Road, Penngrove, CA.

****************

If you are interested in reading more about the body/food connection, I strongly suggest:

THE McDOUGALL PLAN and McDOUGALL'S MEDICINE, by John McDougall, M.D., New Win Publishing, Clinton, New Jersey.

DIET FOR A NEW AMERICA, by John Robbins, Stillpoint Publishing, Walpole, New Hampshire.

****************

For finding out if there is a health risk with any product you use, and also the healthiest choices available, I suggest:

NONTOXIC and NATURAL, by Debra Lynn Dadd, published by Jeremy Tarcher, Inc., Los Angeles, CA.

# RECIPE INDEX